Southern England Poets

Edited By Zak Flint

First published in Great Britain in 2017 by:

Coltsfoot Drive
Peterborough
PE2 9BF
Telephone: 01733 890066
Website: www.youngwriters.co.uk

Book Design by Spencer Hart

SB ISBN 978-1-78624-867-1
Printed and bound in the UK by BookPrintingUK
Website: www.bookprintinguk.com
YB0303B

Foreword

Dear Reader,

Welcome to this book packed full of feathery, furry and scaly friends!

Young Writers' Poetry Safari competition was specifically designed for 5-7 year-olds as a fun introduction to poetry and as a way to think about the world of animals. They could write about pets, exotic animals, dinosaurs and you'll even find a few crazy creatures that have never been seen before! From this starting point, the poems could be as simple or as elaborate as the writer wanted, using imagination and descriptive language.

Given the young age of the entrants, we have tried to include as many poems as possible. Here at Young Writers we believe that seeing their work in print will inspire a love of reading and writing and give these young poets the confidence to develop their skills in the future. Poetry is a wonderful way to introduce young children to the idea of rhyme and rhythm and helps learning and development of communication, language and literacy skills.

These young poets have used their creative writing abilities, sentence structure skills, thoughtful vocabulary and most importantly, their imaginations, to make their poems and the animals within them come alive. I hope you enjoy reading them as much as we have.

Zak Flint

Contents

Farnborough Primary School, Orpington

Katia Maisie Ella Burgess (6) 47
Henry John Brian Attewell (6) 48
Iona Mia Faith Grayson (6) 49
Dannii Louise Doherty (6) 50
Xavier George Reay (6) 51
Scarlett Louise May Wrigley (6) 52
Freya Deal (6) 53
Leon Tozo Kosaka (6) 54
Izzy Scott (6) 55
Penelope Panayiotou (6) 56
Megan Pearce (6) 57
Olivia Beanj (7) 58
Annelise Perry (6) 59

Petworth Primary School, Petworth

Leonardo Velletrani (6) 60
Hayden Griffiths (6) 61
Connie Briggs (5) 62
Charlotte Tooley (6) 63
Evie Mai Thomas (7) 64

Pirton Hill Primary School, Luton

Gabriel Sambou (7) 65
Teodora Chis (7) 66
Mary-Jane Hassan (6) 68
Elias Iacob (6) 70
Chelsey Coombs (6) 72
Andrei-David Apostu (6) 74
Alan Mariat (7) 75
Emiliah Montesardo (6) 76
Lacey Devlin (7) 77
Harmony Dumpleton (7) 78
Ellie-Marie Shury (7) 79
Selina Rama (6) 80
Zara Haque (6) 81
Faraz Irfan (5) 82
Christopher Rice (6) 83
Elijah Akora (5) 84
Jasmine Iqbal (5) 85
Christina Peters (5) 86
Melody Igbinovia (5) 87
Ishaan Minhas (5) 88
Shane Hayles (5) 89

St Margaret Clitherow Catholic Primary School, Bracknell

Caitlin O'Donovan (7) 90
Isabel Parry (7) 92

St Nicolas & St Mary Primary School, Shoreham-By-Sea

Klara Smith (5) 93
Yolanda Allwright (5) 94
Evie Rozario-Johnson (5) 95
Mason James Ollerton (5) 96
Anna Starzacher (5) 97
Isla McArragher (5) 98
Mariana Cate (5) 99
Joshua Ives (5) 100
Sam Alexander (5) 101
Leo Franco-Bittles (6) 102
Hugo Walton (6) 103
Mabel Brookes (6) 104
Sofia De Souza (5) 105
Chelsea Robinson (5) 106
Liberty Fox (5) 107
Emily Bird (5) 108
Mikey Topham (5) 109
George Downes (5) 110
Neve Ladkin (5) 111
Sophie Ball (5) 112
Archie Collins (5) 113
Jack Kelly (5) 114
Cameron McArragher (5) 115
Jensen Jones (5) 116
Luke Samuel Doidge (5) 117
Tristan Storey (5) 118
Olive Wriglesworth (5) 119
Harry Hunt (5) 120
Joshua O'Connor (6) 121

The Poems

Alligator

A n unusual animal
L ikes to be in water
L ikes to chase other animals by the sand
I n the deep blue water
G reen flappy tail
A really big animal
T rying to eat other animals
O n the sand resting
R unning fast across the sand.

Benjamin Leonard (7)
Bredgar CE Primary School, Sittingbourne

Butterfly

B utterfly wings
U nusual animal
T hey have enormous wings
T wirling in the clouds
E xciting animals
R ising in the air
F lying in the sky
L ying in a flower bed
Y oung animal.

Emmie Mia Grzesica (6)
Bredgar CE Primary School, Sittingbourne

Monkey Pig

M onstrous creature
O n the run
N ow endangered
K nightly
E xtremely fascinating
Y ou should see it

P unished by being shot
I ntelligent
G ymnastic animal.

Henry Hinde (7)
Bredgar CE Primary School, Sittingbourne

Polar Bear

P robably cute
O nly fluffy
L ike ice
A re like cold, icy snow
R unning fast or slow

B rave bears
E ars white
A re good
R eally has big colours and babies are soft.

Munashe Tapiwa Elizabeth Mtisi (7)
Bredgar CE Primary School, Sittingbourne

Dolphin

D iving in the deep, dark sea
O n the lookout for sharks
L aughing all the way
P addling in the waves
H er eyes are sparkling
I nteresting animals
N ice dolphin.

Jasmine Annie Boulter (6)
Bredgar CE Primary School, Sittingbourne

Dinosaur

D ifferent animals
I ndestructible animals
N ot plant-eating animals
O nly eats meat
S cary animals
A big animal
U nusual animals
R unning animals.

Finlay Holmes (6)
Bredgar CE Primary School, Sittingbourne

Penguin

P retty furry animal
E specially cute
N ibbling on stinky fish
G iant black penguin
U nder the blue ocean
I n the Arctic
N early ready to eat pongy fish.

Isabelle Pettett (7)
Bredgar CE Primary School, Sittingbourne

Kitten

K ittens are sweet
I can hear a loud miaow
T ired sometimes
T iny and fluffy
E xtremely cute when they purr
N aughty animals when they scratch.

Eviee Lavery (6)
Bredgar CE Primary School, Sittingbourne

Dolphin

D olphins are pretty
O h so wet
L ovely creatures
P urple fish it eats
H ealthy creatures
I n the sea
N aughty creatures.

Konni Louise Lovell (6)
Bredgar CE Primary School, Sittingbourne

Bugslink

B ig legs
U gly creature
G oes click
S unny animal
L eaps in the air
I ndestructible
N aughty
K icking.

Sonny Smith (5)
Bredgar CE Primary School, Sittingbourne

T-Rex

T ramps in the dinosaur woods
R eally likes to hunt brachiosaurus and eats meat
E xtremely dangerous
X -ray shows very small arms.

Frankie Adams (5)

Bredgar CE Primary School, Sittingbourne

Giraffe

G igantic neck
I t is yellow
R ough giraffe
A spotty animal
F luffy
F ast
E xtremely long legs.

Iris Barrett (5)
Bredgar CE Primary School, Sittingbourne

Unicorn

U p in the sky
N ice and fluffy
I t flies
C olourful
O h nice unicorn
R unning
N ice smell.

Emilia Harvey (5)
Bredgar CE Primary School, Sittingbourne

Unicorn

U nicorns have horns
N ice
I n the wood
C ute
O bedient
R un along in the mud
N ot nasty.

Millie Youngs (5)

Bredgar CE Primary School, Sittingbourne

Leopard

L eaping high
E xtremely fast
O rangey fur
P ouncing
A predator
R eady
D otty fur.

Henry Christie (6)
Bredgar CE Primary School, Sittingbourne

Puppies

P uppies are cute
U p bouncing on us
P retty puppy
P erfect puppy
Y elling puppy.

Lily May Stockwell (5)
Bredgar CE Primary School, Sittingbourne

Horse

H airy tail
O bedient
R eally fast
S oft hair
E normous long legs.

Issabell Smith (6)
Bredgar CE Primary School, Sittingbourne

Lion

L ong swishy tail
I n and out of caves
O range coloured fur
N ever scared.

Lola Holmes (5)

Bredgar CE Primary School, Sittingbourne

Dog

D og biscuits
O bedient
G ood sometimes.

Lucas Shilling (5)
Bredgar CE Primary School, Sittingbourne

The Lion

Deadly, pointy teeth.
Large, bushy mane.
Long, bendy tail.
Sharp, scratchy claws.
Loud, frightening roar.
Slimy, wet tongue.
Small black eyes.
Big, smooth body.
Invisible, enormous ears.
Shiny black nose.

Sam Thyer (7)
Charborough Road Primary School, Bristol

All About Elephants

Huge ears.
Gigantic tusks.
Swaying pointy tail.
Long, long tusks.
Bumpy, bumpy back.
Blue, shiny eyes.
Curved, wobbly trunk.
Sharp, pointy nails.
They walk slowly.
They drink with their trunk.

Mia Ponter (6)
Charborough Road Primary School, Bristol

The Elephant

Long, smooth trunk.
Grey, enormous head.
White, sharp tusks.
Soft grey legs.
Beady, small eyes.
Mostly good hearing ears.
Smooth, strong body.
Soft, padded tummy.
Grey, soft tail.

Siona Binu (6)
Charborough Road Primary School, Bristol

The Deadly Lion

Pointy, bladed teeth.
Small, invisible ears.
Smooth, bony legs.
Hooked, scratchy claws.
Golden, skinny body.
Loud, terrifying roar.
Big, bushy mane.
Lions go prowling at night.

Ace Reynolds (6)

Charborough Road Primary School, Bristol

Lion

Bushy, fluffy mane.
Razor-sharp teeth.
Scratchy, dangerous claws.
Smooth, curved tail.
Slimy, pink tongue.
Loud, fierce roar.
Quiet, sneaky feet.
Brown, dirty nose.

Lucy Goddard (6)
Charborough Road Primary School, Bristol

Stompy Elephants

Long, creamy trunk.
Enormous ears.
White sharp tusks.
Strong, stumpy feet.
Dark black, round eyes.
Smooth and soft skin.
Pointy, straight tail.
Noisy, loud trumpet.

Rithvika Sangivi (6)
Charborough Road Primary School, Bristol

The Lion

Razor-sharp teeth.
Big, powerful legs.
Sharp, hooked claws.
Curved, long tail.
Pink, wet tongue.
Golden, bushy mane.
Dark, deadly eyes
Prowling around in the night.

Alexander Phillips (6)
Charborough Road Primary School, Bristol

The Lion

Sharp, razor teeth.
Deadly, dangerous claws.
Bushy, soft tail.
Slimy, sloppy tongue.
Fluffy, furry mane.
Loud, roaring roar.
White, long whiskers.
Brown, wet nose.

Alfie Hayden (7)
Charborough Road Primary School, Bristol

Lion

Fierce, pointy teeth.
Golden, furry mane.
Wiggly, curved tail.
Dangerous, bloody claws.
Loud, deadly roar.
Invisible ears.
Dark, dangerous eyes.

Saptarshi Mondal (6)
Charborough Road Primary School, Bristol

The Elephant

Huge, strong tusks.
Long, curved trunk.
Brown, muddy tail.
Huge, massive ears.
Tiny brown eyes.
Enormous, stumpy feet.
Bumpy brown skin.

Brooke Morton (6)
Charborough Road Primary School, Bristol

The Lion

Sharp, pointy claws.
Furry, soft mane.
Razor, pointy teeth.
Curved, long tail.
Wet, pink tongue.
Big, bumpy back.
Scary orange eyes.

Alexi Jamie Toms (7)
Charborough Road Primary School, Bristol

Elephant

Long, curved trunk.
Huge, massive ears.
Brown, muddy tail.
Huge, strong tusks.
Gigantic, enormous feet.

Mei Callanan (7)
Charborough Road Primary School, Bristol

My Dog Brandy

I have a pet called Brandy who is a dog
She is very old and loves to jog
She is 12 and lives with me in my house.
She is very good and quiet as a mouse.
We like to play together in the garden with
a ball
And sometimes Brandy likes to jump
our wall
She likes to eat delicious doggy treats
But when she is left in the hall she plays
with our shoes.
Brandy is my best friend, I love her loads
I hold her lead on walks to keep her off the
roads.

Archie Richard Nieuwenhuis (6)
Colchester High School, Colchester

Pantiga

I am Pantiga
I live in a zoo eating seeds and spiders
When it is my day off
I like to pop to the park
And scare people
With my loud raaaaas.

My round yellow face has huge red ears
And a green snotty nose
I lick myself with my long bumpy tongue
My thin fluffy body is 10 metres tall
Very, very big and striped.

I ran at people on my yellow feet
Shouting raaaaa.

Oliver O'Daly (5)
Colchester High School, Colchester

Bing The Cat

The furry black cat sat on the mat
Purring away in a deep sleep.
When he wakes up he is playful
And drinks his milk
And eats his fish in a dish.
He loves his house
And chases a mouse all around the garden.
He visits the neighbours
And miaows for favours
As he walks around like a king.
His name is Bing.

Lily Walker (5)
Colchester High School, Colchester

My Funny Fun-Loving Pug

He lives in Puggy Street
And loves his yummy treats.
He is loving and fun
And round as a plum.
He loves chasing his tail
And is a million times faster than a snail.
His bark is funny and loud,
It sounds like a thunder cloud.
My pug is as fast as a bullet train
And loves running in the rain!

James Sherratt (6)
Colchester High School, Colchester

The Fastest Land Animal

Running fast through the grassland,
Far from the jungle.
The speedy cheetah finds his prey in a twinkle.
He does not roar
But he purrs.
His spotty fur helps him hide
In the shadows of the wild.
He is simply the fastest land animal in the world.

Cayden Debrah (7)
Colchester High School, Colchester

Cake Monster Come!

This is a monster made of cake
And it likes to bake.
It never eats meat
But it likes wheat!
It is very poor
And it always wants more.
It likes to eat with its feet.
It always likes to read a book
On a short, black hook!

Martha Evans (6)
Colchester High School, Colchester

The Dogasaurus

There was a dogasaurus
And he had a furry coat.
It was yellow and green
And it fit him like a dream
It didn't keep him warm
Which he didn't think was fair
So he ate a bone leaf sandwich
And grew some extra hair!

Niamh McLellan (6)
Colchester High School, Colchester

Zibby Zebra

Zibby zebra hiding in the marsh
Grazing on lemon grass.
Along came a spotty leopard on the prowl
With a nasty growl.

Camouflaged by stripes,
Hidden by tribes,
Galloped in a flash,
Escaping in a dash.

Dhiara Moodley (5)
Colchester High School, Colchester

The Tiger

Tiger sleeps, then she wakes.
Then she eats a yummy pig and goat.
She then drinks because she is full.
Then she plays because she is bored.
Then she does sit down because she is tired.
And sleepy.

Sophie Rogers (6)
Colchester High School, Colchester

The Flamer

F uriously, the fire-breathing flamer burns
its prey to death
L ooking like a lake of lava
A mazingly acrobatic
M unching madly
E veryone
R un!

Wilfrid Jacobs (6)
Colchester High School, Colchester

Dolphins

Dolphins are clever.
Dolphins are smart.
Dolphins have a big heart.
Dolphins help people
And they love to play.
If I ever see a dolphin
I will shout hooray!

Sofia Skarmoutsou (5)
Colchester High School, Colchester

Silly Steve

Silly Steve is funny.
He likes to run when it's sunny.
He likes to eat people in town
But the people think he is a clown.
He smells like trees
And is full of fleas.
But he is my friend called Steve.

Coral Rain Vye-Parminter (6)
Desmond Anderson Primary School, Crawley

Cutie Iguana

Iguanas are green
And they can swim.

They eat flowers
And have magical powers.

They are little
Cute things.

Evelin Rissling (6)
Desmond Anderson Primary School, Crawley

A Snake Called Jake

Down in the long grass
There was a slithering snake.
He liked to move fast
And Jake was late
For his break.
Jake was a fantastic snake!

Penelope Wotton (6)
Farley Hill Primary School, Reading

The Giraffe In The Bath

Max the giraffe likes a bath,
He plays with bubbles and likes to laugh.
He always eats chocolate treats,
When he dances to the jungle beats.

Megan Handley (5)
Farley Hill Primary School, Reading

Mr Sea Monster's Life

Mr Sea Monster sleeps on seaweed.
That is very strange indeed!
He sleeps in the day
And it's not very comfy.
When he wakes up he gets grumpy.
He goes out at night and steals money
To buy a bed for him and his mummy.
He lives in a cave with his mum and dad
And Dad calls him his little lad!
He wanted to eat people but his mummy wouldn't let him,
So to get the help he needed, he asked his friend Kim.

Katia Maisie Ella Burgess (6)
Farnborough Primary School, Orpington

A Creeper's Life

A creeper starts off very small.
The adult ones are very tall.
A baby creeper can't explode
But the adult ones can explode.
A baby creeper can't eat
So the adult ones feed him.
The adult ones feed themselves!
They both live in a cave
But sometimes they go out and explode people.
Their home cave is a bit of a maze.

Henry John Brian Attewell (6)
Farnborough Primary School, Orpington

A Unicorn In A Poor Home

A unicorn in a grimy house,
It likes to eat meat.
It likes to climb trees.
It's nice and cuddly.
It has sharp teeth.
It is funny.
It likes to do some running.
It lives in the wood.
It is crazy.
It can fly.
It has wings.
It's a magic helping unicorn.
It can help people if they're stuck.

Iona Mia Faith Grayson (6)
Farnborough Primary School, Orpington

Emily The Elephant

Emily the elephant was walking up the road.
Stomp! Stomp! Stomp!
Missing people's toes!
She saw a lake of water
And jumped right in.
Splash! Splash! Splash!
She is soaking everyone!
Emily the elephant was always having fun,
Flapping her eyes all day in the sun.

Dannii Louise Doherty (6)
Farnborough Primary School, Orpington

Shark, Shark

Shark, Shark is really fast,
he will never be seen in the park.
Shark, Shark he will never
be seen in the dark.

Shark, Shark is really hungry,
he hunts around for his next meal.
Shark, Shark is really angry,
don't get eaten Mr Seal!

Xavier George Reay (6)
Farnborough Primary School, Orpington

I Spy An Alligator

I spy an alligator with great big teeth
Who was eating a chicken
Which tasted like beef!
I spy an alligator with spiky ears,
Who was chasing away all the deers.
I spy an alligator who lives in a cave,
He lives in a cave with a friend who is a
Dave.

Scarlett Louise May Wrigley (6)
Farnborough Primary School, Orpington

My Odd Dog

My dog is very odd,
She can fly up to the sky,
Her wings are soft to touch,
I love her very much.

Her favourite place to go
Is the funfair or a show,
Her best food to eat
Is doughnuts and lots of sweets.

Freya Deal (6)

Farnborough Primary School, Orpington

The Sea Monster

The sea monster went for a walk.
He saw his friends and they had a talk
Until they stopped talking and he got hungry.
After that he got angry.
The sea monster found a dead squid
And he was going to eat it but he quit.

Leon Tozo Kosaka (6)
Farnborough Primary School, Orpington

Rosie The Bird Lionaphant

Fiery mane shakes.
Bird wings flap.
Elephant feet stomp.
Snake tail slithers.
Dog body growls.
Rosie is a happy bird lionaphant
Who likes to groove and move.

Izzy Scott (6)
Farnborough Primary School, Orpington

The Helping Butterfly

The helping butterfly is colourful and fun,
It likes to help out everyone.
It likes to take people to the hospital and back.
It likes to keep their babies on track.

Penelope Panayiotou (6)
Farnborough Primary School, Orpington

I'm A Cat In A Hat

I'm called Cat
And I live in a hat.
It's so nice here.
I'm called Cat
And I live in a hat.
'I love the mat,'
Said Cat.

Megan Pearce (6)
Farnborough Primary School, Orpington

The Shock Turtle Horagalles

Shock turtles are smelly,
Some of them have a big belly!
They eat a lot like a pig in a pot!
It has a horn like it's born!

Olivia Beanj (7)
Farnborough Primary School, Orpington

Nibbles

My cat Nibbles likes to purr.
I like to cuddle my cat.
I like to stroke my cat.

Annelise Perry (6)
Farnborough Primary School, Orpington

The Fearsome Shark

One day the fearsome shark swam across corals
And colourful fish.
One day he swam near a sunken boat.
A dark, scary, lonely pirate ship.
One day he swam across the sea
And met a new friend and they played.
One day he saw a bomb falling from the sky
And he swam away faster than he ever had.
One day he swam with his sharp teeth showing,
He saw a big sunken car.

Leonardo Velletrani (6)
Petworth Primary School, Petworth

Hayden And The Cheetah

The cheetah was looking for prey.
Hayden went to pray.
The cheetah found an antelope.
Hayden needed an envelope.
The cheetah was spotty.
Hayden was hungry.
The prey saw the cheetah.
Hayden got a pizza.
The cheetah runs as fast as lightning.
Hayden is very entertaining.
Hayden and the cheetah were attacking.

Hayden Griffiths (6)
Petworth Primary School, Petworth

My Very Special Pet

I have a very special pet.
I am not going to tell you what it is yet.
She has a long fluffy tail,
Once she tried to eat a snail.
She has cone ears and a brown nose.
Daddy says she stinks, but she smells like a rose.
My brother really wants a dog
But I love my cat, Mogg.

Connie Briggs (5)
Petworth Primary School, Petworth

Me And My Unicorn

Me and my magical unicorn...
Fly so high forever and ever,
Land and high forever together.

Me and my unicorn...
Look how we fly,
We fly so high.

Me and my unicorn...
Fly over the sky,
We fly so high, high, high.

Charlotte Tooley (6)
Petworth Primary School, Petworth

Hoppity Rabbits Run, Run, Run

Hoppity rabbit all fluffy and cute.
Hoppity rabbit all adorable and brown.
Hoppity rabbit all safe underground.
Hoppity rabbit keep away from guns.
Hoppity rabbit run, run, run.

Evie Mai Thomas (7)
Petworth Primary School, Petworth

Untitled

I have a long, curly trunk
And I have sharp pointy tusks.
Sometimes I am naughty because I spray water out of my trunk.
I have curved, enormous ears!
My ears are very good to listen with
And my ears are very flappy.
I live in a jungle or you might see me in the zoo.
Usually I will live in the jungle.
I have bumpy, dry skin because it is very hot in Africa.
My back is very strong and I have a huge spine.
I have four huge legs to stamp on branches.
I have long eyelashes.
Did you know I eat delicious, green leaves and fruit?
What am I?

Gabriel Sambou (7)
Pirton Hill Primary School, Luton

Untitled

I have sharp, pointy teeth
Because I use them to eat my prey.
Don't be scared of me unless you're too close to me; if you do that I'll go snap!
You can see me in the jungle, Africa or the zoo.
People usually are scared of me because I have very sharp, pointy teeth.
My favourite food is meat because I am a carnivore.
If you get very close I will eat you!
I could pretend to be a rock, and when people stamp on me I eat them.
When you look at my tongue it looks like slimy grass and my breath smells.
If you feel my back it would feel bumpy and scaly because I am a reptile.
Usually my tail is very long, wiggly and scaly

Because my tail is powerful.
What am I?

My name begins with a C.
Did you know, if you come close to me I can eat you in one bite?
I live near the water because I can go under it to hide;
People or animals think I am a rock.
My favourite food is meat because I am a carnivore.
I am a reptile; usually my skin colour is dark green.
You must be careful because I can find you and come and eat you in one bite!
What am I?

Teodora Chis (7)
Pirton Hill Primary School, Luton

Untitled

I roar loud so that people do not eat my food.
I have a soft, hairy mane.
My tail is as long as a tiger's tail.
Humans call me the king of the jungle
Because I am the loudest animal.
I have sharp, pointy teeth for eating all of my food.
I have long nails, scratching people or scratching my head.
I have gold, brown skin to help me hide in the grass.
My favourite food is meat and I am a carnivore.
I have the reddest tongue out of all the animals.
I have sharp, pointy ears for listening for other lions' roars.
You may see me in the zoo or Africa.

I have four powerful legs for walking.
I love roaring because that's my thing.
I have a swishy thing on my tail
and it is as black as liquorice.
My eyes are wide open to see my prey.
People are scared of me when they visit me at the zoo.
They are scared of me because I roar loud.
When I sleep I dream of eating people which now makes me angry.
What am I?

Mary-Jane Hassan (6)
Pirton Hill Primary School, Luton

Untitled

I begin with the letter L.
You will see me at the zoo because there are lots of animals.
I have a fluffy, cuddly mane so people think I am a teddy bear!
When I am angry I go snap!
My favourite food is meat because I am a carnivore.
I have a short, golden tail so I can tickle people.
I have a long yellow body to help me sneak in the tall green grass.
If you go too close to me I will eat you because I love meat.
You will see that I have a wet, black nose.
You will see that I have black and tiny claws to help me scratch my body.
People call me the king of the jungle.
I have lots of sharp white teeth to help me eat people.

My legs are as long as a snake.
I am a mammal because I have fur on my body.
I have a black bit on the back of the tail.
I have four yellow legs.
What am I?

Elias Iacob (6)

Pirton Hill Primary School, Luton

Untitled

If you come too close I will go snap!
My favourite food is meat
Because sometimes I can go on land or water.
I have scary sharp claws.
I camouflage in the tall, pointy grass.
My claws are as sharp and pointy as my teeth.
You might find me in the zoo and the jungle.
People call me the king of the lizards.
Don't be afraid of me unless you come near me,
I will go snap!
I have sharp, pointy, hard teeth so don't come near me.
I live near water or the zoo.
You never know if I will go snap!
If people think I am a rock I will jump out and say boo.

I have a scaly body up to my tail.
I am a mammal.
What am I?

Chelsey Coombs (6)
Pirton Hill Primary School, Luton

Untitled

You usually find me in Africa or the zoo.
Don't be afraid of me unless you come too close to me because I will roar!
My favourite food is meat because I'm a carnivore.
At the back of my tail is a fluffy part
So if people touch my thing I'll feel it then roar!
Usually people call me the king of the jungle.
My fluffy thing around my head is called a mane.
What am I?
Guess what I am.

Andrei-David Apostu (6)
Pirton Hill Primary School, Luton

Untitled

My mane is brown, fluffy
You meet me at the zoo or the jungle.
Don't be afraid of me unless you come too close to me.
People are afraid of me because I have sharp claws
and big teeth
I will go snap, and eat you!
I have short, yellow, thin legs so I can run fast.
I have a long, yellow, fluffy tail.
My name begins with the letter L.
Do you know who I am?

Alan Mariat (7)
Pirton Hill Primary School, Luton

Untitled

I have pointy teeth because when I get angry I snap.
My long, powerful tail is enormous.
Don't come close to me otherwise I will snap you in my jaws.
Usually I carry my babies down to the river
And birds come and pick out the food.
I have little eyes so I can see.
If I don't see food I will get hungry.
What am I?

Emiliah Montesardo (6)
Pirton Hill Primary School, Luton

Untitled

My mane is fluffy.
Don't be afraid of me unless you come near me!
My teeth are as sharp and pointy as a cat.
I live in a cave.
I have sharp, pointy claws.
My ears are small and tiny.
I have a really long, huge, powerful tail.
I have small, black eyes.
I eat meat because I'm a carnivore.
What am I?

Lacey Devlin (7)
Pirton Hill Primary School, Luton

Untitled

I have sharp, pointy tusks.
I have huge grey ears.
I am a mammal.
I have a huge trunk.
I squirt water out of it sometimes.
Sometimes I eat nuts and leaves.
I have tiny black, beady eyes.
If you come too close to me
I will poke you with my tusks.
My name begins with an E.
What am I?

Harmony Dumpleton (7)
Pirton Hill Primary School, Luton

What Am I?

People are scared of me
Because I have razor-sharp teeth.
My favourite food is brown, bright meat.
My name begins with a C.
I have a powerful, long tail to keep me balanced.
If my teeth are dirty the birds clean my teeth.
My claws are sharp and pointy.
My eyes are tiny like a dot.
What am I?

Ellie-Marie Shury (7)
Pirton Hill Primary School, Luton

Untitled

I am a carnivore because I eat meat.
My voice is as loud as a dinosaur.
I might live in a zoo.
My mane is fluffy as a cat
And my claws are black.
I have tiny legs.
My tongue is pink.
I have a big tummy.
I have pointy ears to hear people.
What am I?

Selina Rama (6)
Pirton Hill Primary School, Luton

Untitled

I am an animal with green skin.
I live in a river,
It has pretty flowers.
I have big, pointy teeth.
I'm slow at running.
I like to live in a river.
I eat spiky grass.
What am I?

Zara Haque (6)
Pirton Hill Primary School, Luton

My Pet

Cat, cat, cat,
Cuddly, cute, crawling.
Cat, cat, cat,
I like cats.

Puppy, puppy, puppy,
Perfect, playing, pounce.
Puppy, puppy, puppy
I love a puppy.

Faraz Irfan (5)
Pirton Hill Primary School, Luton

Untitled

I am green but I am not a lizard.
I have a long and green tail.
I have sharp teeth
So I can bite.
I eat meat but I'm not a tiger.
What am I?

Christopher Rice (6)
Pirton Hill Primary School, Luton

Snake

Snake, snake, snake, snake,
Slithery, slippery, sneaky snake.
Snake, snake, snake, snake,
I like it when they're sneaky.

Elijah Akora (5)
Pirton Hill Primary School, Luton

The Kitten

The kitten crawls.
The kitten has claws.
The kitten runs.
The kitten rolls.
The kitten is in his basket.

Jasmine Iqbal (5)
Pirton Hill Primary School, Luton

Untitled

The cat creeps.
The cat climbs.
The cat scratches.
The cat bites.
The cat fights.

Christina Peters (5)
Pirton Hill Primary School, Luton

The Dog

The dog runs.
The dog drinks.
The dog sleeps.
The dog has sharp claws.

Melody Igbinovia (5)
Pirton Hill Primary School, Luton

Untitled

Snakes, snakes, snakes
I don't like snakes
Because they are slithery.

Ishaan Minhas (5)
Pirton Hill Primary School, Luton

The Tiger

The tiger trips.
The tiger trains.
The tiger runs.
The tiger roars.

Shane Hayles (5)
Pirton Hill Primary School, Luton

Fun In The Jungle

Deep in the jungle
The palm trees hang.
Giraffes with short necks,
Puffins with long necks, what a bungle!
Gorillas beating their chests with a great big bang.

Branches hang down low
For the monkeys to swing from vine to vine.
So many places I don't know where to go!
Rhinos balancing carefully on a line.

The lions roaring up to the bright blue sky.
The lioness sitting there
With her deep brown eyes;
Look at her beautiful golden hair!

Crocodile's gliding in the forbidden river
Looking for food to eat.

He caught sight of some slimy liver
And trudged along with his enormous feet.

Look at all the views!
Look at the waterfall crash down below.
So many fun things to do,
The jungle is a fun place; now you know!

Caitlin O'Donovan (7)
St Margaret Clitherow Catholic Primary School, Bracknell

Reater Cheetah

In a desert there was a cheetah who could run a metre
Faster than a snail that could cross a nail
Cheetah Reater was no better
Because she was the prettiest eater.

Cheetah Reater had loads of spots
And so she gave loads of shots.
Every day she goes to the waterfall
To get to the shopping mall.
She eats enough fish to help her swish
Through the trees, faster than her fleas.

Isabel Parry (7)
St Margaret Clitherow Catholic Primary School, Bracknell

My Kitten

She is as cute as a rabbit.
She is as grey as an elephant.
She has pointy ears.
She has grey and black spots.
She is playful.
Her food is in tins.
She is a kitten.

Klara Smith (5)
St Nicolas & St Mary Primary School, Shoreham-By-Sea

Who Am I?

I am as small as a hamster.
I have three claws.
I have small legs.
I have black stripes like a zebra.
I am as fast as a cheetah.
Who am I?
I am a velociraptor.

Yolanda Allwright (5)
St Nicolas & St Mary Primary School, Shoreham-By-Sea

My Goldfish

He is as shiny as a trophy.
He is as swishy as a plant.
He is as small as a ladybird.
He is as cuddly as a bunny.
He is as fluffy as a bird.
He is a goldfish.

Evie Rozario-Johnson (5)
St Nicolas & St Mary Primary School, Shoreham-By-Sea

Untitled

My dog is as cute as a donkey
And I love her so much.
She licks my dad's head.
She is adorable.
She is as cute as a cat.
She is as crazy as a hippo.

Mason James Ollerton (5)
St Nicolas & St Mary Primary School, Shoreham-By-Sea

Who Am I?

I am as fluffy as a bear.
I am as cuddly as a monkey.
I am as cute as a kitten.
I am as black and white as a zebra.
Who am I?
I am a penguin.

Anna Starzacher (5)
St Nicolas & St Mary Primary School, Shoreham-By-Sea

Who Am I?

I am as pretty as a princess.
I have four legs like a giraffe.
I am as black as a gorilla.
I am as fluffy as a cloud.
Who am I?
I am a cat.

Isla McArragher (5)
St Nicolas & St Mary Primary School, Shoreham-By-Sea

Who Am I?

I am as strong as a gorilla.
I am as pretty as a princess.
I am as soft as a cloud.
I am cute like a puppy.
Who am I?
I am a kitten.

Mariana Cate (5)
St Nicolas & St Mary Primary School, Shoreham-By-Sea

My Tarantula

He is as furry as a massive dog.
He is as poisonous as a scorpion.
He has eyes as fiery as the big bad mouse.
He is a tarantula...

Joshua Ives (5)
St Nicolas & St Mary Primary School, Shoreham-By-Sea

Who Am I?

I am as cute as a rabbit.
I have four legs.
I am as nice as a bear.
I am as cute as a rabbit.
Who am I?
I am Sam's cat.

Sam Alexander (5)
St Nicolas & St Mary Primary School, Shoreham-By-Sea

My Bat

He is as scary as a dragon.
He is as black as a black horse.
He is as funny as a rabbit.
He is as flappy as a bird.
He is a bat.

Leo Franco-Bittles (6)
St Nicolas & St Mary Primary School, Shoreham-By-Sea

Who Am I?

I am as fierce as a cheetah.
I am as small as a hamster.
I have teeth like a tiger.
Who am I?
I am a velociraptor.

Hugo Walton (6)
St Nicolas & St Mary Primary School, Shoreham-By-Sea

Who Am I?

I am as fierce as a tiger.
I am as fluffy as a kitten.
I am as stripy as a zebra.
Who am I?
I am a badger.

Mabel Brookes (6)
St Nicolas & St Mary Primary School, Shoreham-By-Sea

Who Am I?

I am as fluffy as a bear.
I am fast as a cheetah.
I have a wet nose like a dog.
Who am I?
I am a kitten.

Sofia De Souza (5)
St Nicolas & St Mary Primary School, Shoreham-By-Sea

Who Am I?

I am fluffy as a bear.
I am spotty like a leopard.
I am as cute as a hamster.
Who am I?
I am a kitten.

Chelsea Robinson (5)
St Nicolas & St Mary Primary School, Shoreham-By-Sea

Who Am I?

I am as tough as a gorilla.
I run fast like a cheetah.
I live in snow.
Who am I?
I am a snow leopard.

Liberty Fox (5)

St Nicolas & St Mary Primary School, Shoreham-By-Sea

Who Am I?

I am as black as a gorilla.
I have four legs like a horse.
I like bones.
Who am I?
I am a dog.

Emily Bird (5)
St Nicolas & St Mary Primary School, Shoreham-By-Sea

My Zebra

He is as big as a pumpkin.
He is as big as a pumpkin.
He is as stripy as a tiger.
He's a zebra.

Mikey Topham (5)
St Nicolas & St Mary Primary School, Shoreham-By-Sea

My Dog

He is as soft as a pillow.
He is as big as a lion.
He is as cuddly as a teddy.
He is a nice dog.

George Downes (5)
St Nicolas & St Mary Primary School, Shoreham-By-Sea

My Panda

He is as lovely as a cat.
He is as great as a dog.
He is as adorable as a snake.
He is a panda!

Neve Ladkin (5)
St Nicolas & St Mary Primary School, Shoreham-By-Sea

Who Am I?

I am as fast as a mouse.
I am as cute as a bunny.
Who am I?
I am a mighty eagle.

Sophie Ball (5)
St Nicolas & St Mary Primary School, Shoreham-By-Sea

My Mystery Animal

He is as cute as a white cat.
He is as fluffy as Chewbacca.
He is as soft as a cloud.

Archie Collins (5)
St Nicolas & St Mary Primary School, Shoreham-By-Sea

Untitled

My monkey is cheeky.
He is fast like a cheetah.
He eats bananas, then slides on them.

Jack Kelly (5)
St Nicolas & St Mary Primary School, Shoreham-By-Sea

Who Am I?

I am as fluffy as a cat.
I have four legs like a lion.
Who am I?
I am a dog.

Cameron McArragher (5)
St Nicolas & St Mary Primary School, Shoreham-By-Sea

My Penguin

He is as fluffy as a swan duckling.
He is as black as a panther.
He is a penguin.

Jensen Jones (5)
St Nicolas & St Mary Primary School, Shoreham-By-Sea

My Gorilla

He is as strong as a lion.
He is as great as a plane.
He is as hairy as a mouse.

Luke Samuel Doidge (5)
St Nicolas & St Mary Primary School, Shoreham-By-Sea

Who Am I?

I am as fluffy as a bear.
I am as stripy as a zebra.
Who am I?
I am a cat.

Tristan Storey (5)
St Nicolas & St Mary Primary School, Shoreham-By-Sea

What Am I?

I am as cute as a kitten
I am as bouncy as a frog
Who am I?
I am a rabbit.

Olive Wriglesworth (5)
St Nicolas & St Mary Primary School, Shoreham-By-Sea

Who Am I?

I can fly like a bird.
I am as brown as a tree.
Who am I?
I am an eagle.

Harry Hunt (5)
St Nicolas & St Mary Primary School, Shoreham-By-Sea

What Am I?

He is as furry as a bear
He is as scary as a monster
It's a tarantula.

Joshua O'Connor (6)
St Nicolas & St Mary Primary School, Shoreham-By-Sea

My Unicorn

My unicorn is as cuddly
As a teddy bear
And I love her.

Annabelle Underhill (5)

St Nicolas & St Mary Primary School, Shoreham-By-Sea

The Best Poem I Can Write

The crocodile is as fierce as a beast.
The crocodile's teeth are as sharp as a knife.
The crocodile is as scary as a monster.
The crocodile is as crazy as a conker.
The crocodile is as slow as a slug.
The crocodile is as sneaky as a fox.
The crocodile is as hungry as my dad.
The crocodile is as curious as a monkey.
The crocodile is as crunchy as a clam.

William Coombes (6)
The Daiglen School, Buckhurst Hill

The Soft Lion

The lion's roar is as loud as a thunderstorm.
The lion's mane is as soft as a pillow.
The lion's claws are as sharp as a needle.
The lion is as sleepy as a baby.
The lion's tail is as long as a snake.
The lion is as fast as a cheetah.
The lion is as hot as a cup of tea.
The lion is as sneaky as a fox.

Sofia Georgiou (6)
The Daiglen School, Buckhurst Hill

The Fierce, Scary Crocodile

The crocodile was scary
And weary after attacking.
Her eyes were as beady and small
As a human being's thumb!
The crocodile's tooth was as sharp
As a shark's canine.
The crocodile's leg was as small
As a tyrannosaurus rex's legs.
The crocodile eats pounds full of fish
All in one gulp!

Renee Bhargava (6)
The Daiglen School, Buckhurst Hill

The Really Big Crocodile

The crocodile wants to eat meat.
The crocodile is green, it is mean
Because it wants tea.
The crocodile does not like bees
But loves cheese.
The crocodile has a nail in his tail.
The plan failed to rescue the male crocodile.
The crocodile caught the rat with a bat.

Abraham Warsi (6)
The Daiglen School, Buckhurst Hill

The Male Lion

The lion is male and it has a tail.
The lion is as loud as bombs dropping.
His skin is as warm as a fireball.
His teeth are as strong as a brick.
The lion sat on a mat
And had a huge nap.
His fur is very furry
And he is very purry.

George Worwood (7)
The Daiglen School, Buckhurst Hill

The King Lion

The lazy, fierce lion is as bony as a fish.
He is old and cold.
He is smelly and has a big belly.
He is proud as an eagle.
He lives in the middle of the road he knows.
When he smells food, that's when he goes.

Amaan Khoda (6)

The Daiglen School, Buckhurst Hill

The Ugly, Fierce And Mischievous Crocodile

The ugly, fierce and mischievous crocodile
Hid behind a tree
And jumped out and ate
His prey in his deep, dark cave.
When he chewed his prey he said, 'Hooray!'
And he was the meanest crocodile in town.

Niam Lad (6)

The Daiglen School, Buckhurst Hill

The Crocodile Who Went To The Swamp

The crocodile went to the swamp.
His scales are as bumpy as a log.
His legs are as small as a turtle's.
He eats big fish.
The crocodile is as fierce as a dragon!
His teeth are as sharp as a knife.

Felix Lammin (7)
The Daiglen School, Buckhurst Hill

The Weary Lion

A lion's fur is as cosy as a blanket.
A lion's roar is as loud as a firework.
A lion's tooth is as sharp as a blade.
A lion sat on a mat
And had a nap.

Jamie Nathan Shellard (6)
The Daiglen School, Buckhurst Hill

The Scary Sleepy Lion

The lion is very sleepy.
He is also very creepy.
He is as soft as clouds,
Sneaky and sleepy.
He is very sly.
He roars loudly.
He is very scary.

Margaux Scout Swain (6)
The Daiglen School, Buckhurst Hill

Best Unicorn

A unicorn is pretty.
A unicorn is colourful.
A unicorn is extraordinary.
A unicorn is a friend.
A unicorn is fun.
A unicorn is nice.
A unicorn is smiley.
My unicorn is fun.
My unicorn is beautiful.
If a unicorn had wings
It could fly up to the sky.
A unicorn is not real.
Some people might believe that it is real.
If a unicorn is real I think I want to see one.
I think a unicorn is afraid of you.

Megan Elizabeth Frank (6)
Wessex Primary School, Maidenhead

Mighty King Of The Jungle

The lion standing over there is watching you,
He's mighty big and strong.
He looks quite cute and friendly
But if you think that you are wrong!
He's the king of the jungle.

He's looking for his dinner,
If there's a race he will be the winner!
He's the king of the jungle.

Charging across the grassy African plain
He shakes his fluffy golden mane.
He's the king of the jungle.

He's a carnivore,
He needs meat for his dinner,
If he doesn't find any he'll get thinner and thinner.
He's the king of the jungle.

He kills his prey to eat once a day
With sharp claws and sharp jaws,
Don't stand in his way,
He's the king of the jungle.

He will catch his prey with pride and care,
So try and stroke him if you dare!
He's the king of the jungle.

Sophia Todd (6)
Wessex Primary School, Maidenhead

Pippa's Day

I know a dog and Pippa is her name;
Playing fetch is her favourite game.
She loves walks in the park
But like me she doesn't like the dark.
Pippa is brown and white
And very small.
Pippa loves playing with a ball,
She barks a lot when at home,
Especially when she is left alone.

Theo Lane (6)
Wessex Primary School, Maidenhead

Red Pandas

Red pandas are fluffy,
They climb up trees
With their really shiny claws
To eat lots of leaves
Which are tasty, for their tea.

They share them with their friends,
They look very cuddly
And I wish they could cuddle me.
Red pandas.

Aiden Siddons (6)
Wessex Primary School, Maidenhead

The Lion

The lion is big.
The lion is strong.
The lion is fast.
The lion is long.
He's yellow and ginger.
His colour is bright.
A big wide mane all fluffy and nice.
He really is a beautiful sight.

Talea Moraitis (6)
Wessex Primary School, Maidenhead

My Puppy

P uppy is cute and out he goes
U p the stairs puppy goes
P uppy has a cute face and smile
P uppy jumps into a pile of hay
Y ummy treats that he likes to eat.

Leyla Akkus (7)
Wessex Primary School, Maidenhead

Sarlacc

In the desert on Tatooine,
Scary Sarlacc
Spiky and mean.

Scary Sarlacc
Stings like a bee
Please, scary Sarlacc
Don't eat me.

Charlie Robertson (6)
Wessex Primary School, Maidenhead

Leopard

L ovely pet
E nergetic and excellent
O verjoyed to be here
P layful
A dorable
R unning
D elightful.

Ellie Roberts (6)
Wessex Primary School, Maidenhead

The Creepers

The creepers never sleep.
They are always on the creep.
They are big and small
And some are very tall.
But they all have small feet.

Josh Kent (7)
Wessex Primary School, Maidenhead

Unicorn

U nbelievable
N ice
I ncredible
C olourful
O bedient
R ainbow coloured
N eat.

Lexi McDermott (6)
Wessex Primary School, Maidenhead

Lion

L ikes to eat meat
I t is very fierce
O nly eats people when it is angry
N ever try to cuddle one.

Lexie Hayes (7)
Wessex Primary School, Maidenhead

The Monkey Jumps On The Car

Her ears are pointy.
She is very, very funny.
And she is very, very jumpy.

Every time a car comes past
The monkey jumps on it.
When someone puts down their window
She turns around and...
Wiggles her tail.

Ella Armour (5)

White Cliffs Primary College Of The Arts, Dover

Untitled

What goes moooo? Cow!
What goes mememem? Sheep!
What goes choo, choo, choo? Train.
What goes roar, roar? Lion.
What goes help? Mouse.
What goes aaa? People.

Lexi Jane Reynolds (5)
White Cliffs Primary College Of The Arts, Dover